D0489365

how to live a
happy
life

how to live a
happy
life

ONE HUNDRED WAYS TO
A JOYFUL LIFE

An Hachette UK Company
www.hachette.co.uk

First published as *Everyday Happiness* in 2016
by Bounty Books,
a division of Octopus Publishing Group Ltd
Carmelite House
50 Victoria Embankment
London, EC4Y 0DZ

Published in 2018 by Bounty Books, a division of
Octopus Publishing Group Ltd

www.octopusbooks.co.uk

Copyright © Octopus Publishing Group Ltd 2016,
2018

All rights reserved. No part of this work may
be reproduced or utilized in any form or by
any means, electronic or mechanical, including
photocopying, recording or by any information
storage and retrieval system, without the prior
written permission of the publisher.

ISBN: 978-0-7537-3281-6

A CIP catalogue record for this book is available
from the British Library

Printed and bound in China

10 9 8 7 6 5 4 3 2 1

Publisher: Lucy Pessell
Designer: Lisa Layton
Editor: Sarah Vaughan
Production Controller: Beata Kibil
Images: Shutterstock/Irtsya

INTRODUCTION

Happy (adjective):
1. *Feeling or showing pleasure or contentment.*
2. *Fortunate or convenient.*

"They felt happy when they saw the sun rise."

Increasingly, scientists and philosophers are exploring what happiness is and how we can achieve it. If happiness were a formula, it would perhaps look something like this:

Gratitude + love + mindfulness
+ achievable goals = happiness

…with variations colored by subjective opinion. One thing most happiness researchers do seem to agree on is that happiness is a choice; something that comes from within and that you can strive to achieve, regardless of your circumstances.

How to Live a Happy Life provides the perfect pick-me-up for days when you're in need of a positive boost.

Here you will find an eclectic mix of inspirational quotes; some are life affirming, others thought-provoking or joyous, but all of them promote happiness.

Along with these daily inspirations are ideas and exercises to help you cultivate contentment.

Many of these tips involve taking just a few minutes out of your day, yet it's these small steps taken each day that will help set you on the path to happiness.

Use this book as your guide, inspiration and motivation to make this your happiest year yet.

MAKE A
GRATITUDE JAR

Decorate an empty jar, to be filled throughout the year with notes
about good things that happen. Don't let these good things pass by
unnoticed, however small they may be.

"It's a helluva start, being able to recognize what makes you happy."

– LUCILLE BALL

"It isn't what you have, or who you are, or where you are, or what you are doing that makes you happy or unhappy. It is what you think about."

– DALE CARNEGIE

"We tend to forget that happiness doesn't come as a result of getting something we don't have, but rather of recognizing and appreciating what we do have."

– FREDERICK KEONIG

EXERCISE

Exercise increases endorphins and other feel-good brain chemicals, so get moving today. Research suggests that the mood benefits of just 20 minutes of exercise can last for 12 hours. In fact exercise has such a profound effect on our happiness and wellbeing that it is an effective strategy for overcoming depression.

"Some cause
happiness wherever
they go; others
whenever they go."

– OSCAR WILDE

"A man cannot be comfortable without his own approval."

– MARK TWAIN

"Happiness is
not something ready-
made. It comes from
your own actions."

– DALAI LAMA

REMEMBER, MONEY CAN'T BUY HAPPINESS

Research shows that once income climbs above the poverty level, more money brings very little extra happiness. Yet still so many of us strive to accumulate monetary wealth. This pursuit of "stuff" will never bring enduring happiness.

"Very little is needed to make a happy life; it is all within yourself, in your way of thinking."

– MARCUS AURELIUS

"Twenty years from now you will
be more disappointed by the things
that you didn't do than by the ones
you did do.
So throw off the bowlines.
Sail away from the safe harbor.
Catch the trade winds in your sails.
Explore. Dream. Discover."

– MARK TWAIN

"If you spend your whole life waiting for the storm, you'll never enjoy the sunshine."

– MORRIS WEST

"Most people are about as happy as they make up their minds to be."

- ABRAHAM LINCOLN

SLEEP MORE

We all know that sleep helps the body to repair itself, increases focus and concentration, but did you know it also plays an important role in happiness? Scientific studies have proven that sleep affects our sensitivity to negative emotions. So if you want to be more resilient, get an early night.

"To be kind to all, to like many and love a few, to be needed and wanted by those we love, is certainly the nearest we can come to happiness."

– MARY STUART

"Happiness consists of living each day as if it were the first day of your honeymoon and the last day of your vacation."

– LEO TOLSTOY

"I believe compassion to be one of the few things we can practise that will bring immediate and long-term happiness to our lives."

– DALAI LAMA

"Each morning when I open my eyes I say to myself: I, not events, have the power to make me happy or unhappy today. I can choose which it shall be. Yesterday is dead, tomorrow hasn't arrived yet. I have just one day, today, and I'm going to be happy in it."

– GROUCHO MARX

SPEND TIME
WITH FAMILY

Top of the list of regrets expressed late in life is not spending enough time with family. Quality family time together is one major key to happiness.

"A table, a chair, a bowl of fruit and a violin; what else does a man need to be happy?"

– ALBERT EINSTEIN

"This planet has — or rather had — a problem, which was this: most of the people living on it were unhappy for pretty much all of the time. Many solutions were suggested for this problem, but most of these were largely concerned with the movement of small green pieces of paper, which was odd because on the whole it wasn't the small green pieces of paper that were unhappy."

– DOUGLAS ADAMS

GET OUTSIDE

Make the time to go outdoors today, even if just for 20 minutes in your lunch break. Studies show that fresh air boosts positivity and improves happiness levels.

"Life is really
simple, but we
insist on making
it complicated."

– CONFUCIUS

GET IN TOUCH WITH AN OLD FRIEND

Why not contact an old friend who you haven't seen for a while? Don't let good friendships slip away just because life is busy. Make the effort to take ten minutes out of your day to write an email or a letter, or pick up the phone.

"If more of us valued food and cheer and song above hoarded gold, it would be a merrier world."

– J.R.R. TOLKIEN

"Thousands of candles can be lighted from a single candle, and the life of the candle will not be shortened. Happiness never decreases by being shared."

– BUDDHA

"A well-developed sense of humor is the pole that adds balance to your steps as you walk the tightrope of life."

– WILLIAM ARTHUR WARD

EXPRESS YOURSELF

Many of us suppress our feelings in order to keep the peace with others. This is so restrictive and can lead to a mediocre existence. Have the strength to express your feelings. Have the courage to live the life you want to.

"Learn to let go.
That is the key to
happiness."

– BUDDHA

"The grass is always greener where you water it."

– UNKNOWN

"The moments of happiness we enjoy take us by surprise. It is not that we seize them, but that they seize us."

– ASHLEY MONTAGU

HELP OTHERS

Hold open the door for someone, let a car out in traffic, deliver a homemade dinner to a friend, do some gardening for a neighbor in need, smile at a stranger…However small your gesture, it can make a huge difference to someone else's day, and the lovely side effect of this…you will feel happier!

"Don't cry
because it's over,
smile because it
happened."

– DR. SEUSS

"Count your age by friends, not years. Count your life by smiles, not tears."

- JOHN LENNON

"Happiness is not so much in having as sharing. We make a living by what we get, but we make a life by what we give."

– NORMAN MACEWAN

"It is only possible to live happily ever after on a day-to-day basis."

– MARGARET BONANNO

SMILE

Several studies have shown that smiling may not just be an outward manifestation of a happy feeling. It may actually be able to cause a happy feeling.

"Sometimes your joy is the source of your smile, but sometimes your smile can be the source of your joy."

– THÍCH NHẤT HẠNH

Let yourself be happy.

"All seasons are beautiful for the person who carries happiness within."

– HORACE FRIESS

HAPPINESS IS
A CHOICE

The happiest people do not seek happiness in other people or possessions. They are not held hostage by circumstance. They understand that happiness comes from within and it is a choice. Today, whatever is going on in your life, choose happiness.

"The best way to
cheer yourself
is to try to cheer
somebody else up."

– MARK TWAIN

"The foolish man seeks happiness in the distance, the wise grows it under his feet."

– JAMES OPPENHEIM

"The greatest part
of our happiness
depends on our
dispositions, not our
circumstances."

– MARTHA WASHINGTON

"The grand essentials of happiness are: something to do, something to love, and something to hope for."

– ALLAN K. CHALMERS

BE GRATEFUL

Let gratitude be your first thought in the morning and your last thought before you go to bed.

"For every minute you are angry, you lose sixty seconds of happiness."

– RALPH WALDO EMERSON

"Be yourself;
everyone else is
already taken."

– OSCAR WILDE

SURROUND YOURSELF WITH HAPPY PEOPLE

Happiness is catching — being around contented people boosts your own mood. And by being happy yourself, you give something back to them. One big reciprocal circle of happy.

"You will never be happy if you continue to search for what happiness consists of.
You will never live if you are looking for the meaning of life."

– ALBERT CAMUS

PLAN A TRIP

Even if you can't go on vacation for a while, plan ahead for a time when you can. It's often the anticipation of a positive event — not the event itself — that makes us happiest.

"'Well,' said Pooh, 'What I like best,'
and then he had to stop and think.
Because although eating honey was
a very good thing to do, there was a
moment just before you began to eat it
which was better than when you were,
but he didn't know what it was called."

– A.A. MILNE

"When one door of happiness closes, another opens; but often we look so long at the closed door that we do not see the one which has been opened for us."

– HELEN KELLER

"When all your desires are distilled;
You will cast just two votes:
To love more,
And be happy."

– RUMI

"The summit of happiness is reached when a person is ready to be what he is."

– DESIDERIUS ERASMUS

MEDITATE

Rewire your brain for happiness by meditating. Meditation clears the mind and calms you. It is often cited as the single most effective way to live a happier life.

"The pursuit of happiness is a most ridiculous phrase; if you pursue happiness you'll never find it."

– C. P. SNOW

"Those who bring sunshine into the lives of others, cannot keep it from themselves."

– JAMES M. BARRIE

TRY SOMETHING NEW

Challenge and novelty are key elements of happiness. Do something today that you've never done before.

"Your happiness
is a gift because it
literally brings out
the best in you."

– ROBERT HOLDEN

"Happiness depends upon ourselves."

– ARISTOTLE

"That is happiness;
to be dissolved
into something
completely great."

– WILLA CATHER

"We all live with the objective of being happy; our lives are all different and yet the same."

– ANNE FRANK

"Every morning, when we wake up, we have twenty-four brand new hours to live. What a precious gift! We have the capacity to live in a way that these twenty-four hours will bring peace, joy and happiness to ourselves and others."

– THÍCH NHẤT HẠNH

"Happiness is letting go of what you think your life is supposed to look like and celebrating it for everything that it is."

– MANDY HALE

"Happiness is like a butterfly; the more you chase it, the more it will elude you, but if you turn your attention to other things, it will come and sit softly on your shoulder..."

– HENRY DAVID THOREAU

LIVE IN THE MOMENT

Take 10 minutes out of your day for a mindfulness meditation. Being mindful means living in the moment, noticing what's going on both within our minds and in our immediate surroundings. It involves a gentle, non-judgemental acceptance of thoughts.

"Do not look back on happiness or dream of it in the future. You are only sure of today; do not let yourself be cheated out of it."

– HENRY WARD BEECHER

"The best day of your life is the one on which you decide your life is your own. No apologies or excuses. No one to lean on, rely on, or blame. The gift is yours — it is an amazing journey — and you alone are responsible for the quality of it. This is the day your life really begins."

– BOB MOAWAD

"One gets a bad habit of being unhappy."

– GEORGE ELIOT

HUG

Today give someone a genuine warm hug.
They'll hug you back and you'll both feel great!

HAVE A LAUGH

Laughter improves health, mood, and social skills and is
now even used as a therapy (laughter yoga was started in Mumbai by
Dr. Madan Katarina, who is now happily running over 5,000 clubs
worldwide). So raise those endorphin levels and have a good chuckle.

"You cannot live your life to please others. The choice must be yours."

– LEWIS CARROLL

DANCE

Dance with carefree abandon.
Dance like nobody's watching.
Dance until you're sweating.
Dance until you can't wipe the smile off your face.

"There is no such thing as a problem without a gift for you in its hands. You seek problems because you need their gifts."

– RICHARD BACH

"If you want to be happy,
set a goal that commands your
thoughts, liberates your energy, and
inspires your hopes."

– ANDREW CARNEGIE

LISTEN

Instead of waiting to jump in to a conversation, slow down and really listen to what somebody is telling you. You will feel a better connection to the person you are talking to if you understand their views. And a better connection equals increased levels of contentment within a relationship.

"The supreme happiness of life is the conviction that we are loved."

– VICTOR HUGO

"It is not easy to find happiness in ourselves, and it is not possible to find it elsewhere."

– AGNES REPPLIER

"We can travel a long way and do many things, but our deepest happiness is not born from accumulating new experiences. It is born from letting go of what is unnecessary, and knowing ourselves to be always at home."

– SHARON SALZBERG

SURROUND YOURSELF BY PEOPLE YOU LOVE

Our happiness levels increase when we are in the presence of people we love, so spend as much time as possible with the people you love. Simple!

"Try to make at least one person happy every day, and then in ten years you may have made three thousand, six hundred and fifty persons happy, or brightened a small town by your contribution to the fund of general enjoyment."

– SYDNEY SMITH

"The good life, as I conceive it, is a happy life. I do not mean that if you are good you will be happy; I mean that if you are happy you will be good."

– BERTRAND RUSSELL

"Most of us would be upset if we were accused of being 'silly.' But the word 'silly' comes from the old English word 'selig,' and its literal definition is 'to be blessed, happy, healthy, and prosperous.'"

– ZIG ZIGLAR

MAKE A
GRATITUDE LIST

Today, write down three good things that happened to you. It doesn't matter how small a thing it was. Anything that made you feel good at the time or that you're grateful for. This is a great way to ground yourself in what you love about your life. Grateful people are inevitably more fulfilled, contented, and happy.

"Happiness, it seems to me, consists of two things: first, in being where you belong, and second — and best — in comfortably going through everyday life, that is, having had a good night's sleep and not being hurt by new shoes."

– THEODOR FONTANE

"Ever since happiness heard your name, it has been running through the streets trying to find you."

– HAFIZ OF PERSIA

"I had rather have a fool to make me merry than experience to make me sad."

– WILLIAM SHAKESPEARE

"I've learned that people will forget what you said, people will forget what you did, but people will never forget how you made them feel."

– MAYA ANGELOU

FAKE IT 'TIL YOU FEEL IT

Feelings follow actions. Today, if you're feeling low, act cheery. If you feel anger toward somebody, do something thoughtful for them and notice how this softens your anger.

"If you look to others for fulfillment, you will never be fulfilled. If your happiness depends on money, you will never be happy with yourself. Be content with what you have; rejoice in the way things are. When you realize there is nothing lacking, the world belongs to you."

– LAO TZU

"Happiness can be found even in the darkest of times, when one only remembers to turn on the light."

– J. K. ROWLING

"Tension is who you
think you should be,
relaxation is who
you are."

– CHINESE PROVERB

"The art of living lies less in eliminating our troubles than growing with them."

– BERNARD M. BARUCH

"For me it is sufficient to have a corner by my hearth, a book, and a friend, and a nap undisturbed by creditors or grief."

– ANDRÉS FERNÁNDEZ DE ANDRADA

FORGIVE

According to a rapidly growing body of research, holding a grudge and
nursing grievances can affect physical as well as mental health. So learn
how to forgive. Try to let go of past hurts. Move on with compassion in
your heart and your head held high.

"Happiness cannot be traveled to, owned, earned, worn, or consumed. Happiness is the spiritual experience of living every minute with love, grace, and gratitude."

– DENIS WAITLEY

"Happiness is not a station you arrive at, but a manner of traveling."

– MARGARET LEE RUNBECK

"Focus on the journey, not the destination. Joy is found not in finishing an activity but in doing it."

– GREG ANDERSON

"You never regret being kind."

– NICOLE SHEPHERD

AN ACT OF
RANDOM KINDNESS

Maybe buy a stranger their coffee, let someone jump the line ahead of
you, send anonymous flowers, buy someone a lottery ticket…then revel
in the warm glow it brings you.

"Forgiveness does not change the past, but it does enlarge the future."

– PAUL BOESE

"In our lives, change is unavoidable, loss is unavoidable. In the adaptability and ease with which we experience change, lies our happiness and freedom."

– BUDDHA

"Reflect upon your present blessings, of which every man has many — not on your past misfortunes, of which all men have some."

– CHARLES DICKENS

"He who lives in harmony with himself lives in harmony with the universe."

– MARCUS AURELIUS

DECLUTTER

Start with one room or area in your house and focus on decluttering. Your mind will feel calmer and clearer for having done this.

"If you want others to be happy, practise compassion.
If you want to be happy, practise compassion."

– DALAI LAMA

"Happiness is not having what you want. It is appreciating what you have."

– UNKNOWN

"We make a living by what we get, we make a life by what we give."

– WINSTON CHURCHILL

"There is no stress in the world, only people thinking stressful thoughts and then acting on them."

- WAYNE DYER

"There is only one thing more painful than learning from experience and that is not learning from experience."

– ARCHIBALD MACLEISH

"Anything in life that we don't accept will simply make trouble for us until we make peace with it."

– SHAKTI GAWAIN

"Do what you have always done and you'll get what you have always got."

– SUE KNIGHT

BE PROACTIVE IN YOUR RELATIONSHIPS

Particularly in regards to your partner. There is plenty of evidence to suggest that relationships, particularly marriages, decline over time. Don't switch to autopilot mode. Make an effort to engage. Today and every day.

"Good friends, good books, and a sleepy conscience: this is the ideal life."

– MARK TWAIN

"Happiness is the experience of loving life. Being happy is being in love with that momentary experience. And love is looking at someone or even something and seeing the absolute best in him, her, or it. Love is happiness with what you see. So love and happiness really are the same thing... just expressed differently."

– ROBERT MCPHILLIPS

EMBRACE
THE POSITIVE

Focus on embracing everything positive that happens to you today, however small that thing may be. For anything negative that happens, turn it into a positive. There's always a new way of looking at something, a way to put a positive spin on it.